ANDROID PHONES USER GUIDE FOR BEGINNERS

The Complete and Illustrated Manual for Beginners and Seniors to Master Android Phones

By

Alston Wallace

Copyright © 2021 Alston Wallace,

All rights reserved

Android Phones User Guide for Beginners

TABLE OF CONTENTS

Introduction **4**
Getting Started... **6**
    Navigating on an Android device 6
        Home button 8
        How to change the look of your home screen 9
        How you can set up your new Phone. 12
        Google Assistant integration 14
        Google Pay...16
        Google Play..17
        The Notification Panel 19
        The Status Bar 20
        How to Send a Text Message on Your Android Phone 21
        How to Make and Receive Calls on an Android Phone.......23
        How you can receive a call on your Android Phone 30
        How to save a contact on your Android phone 35
        How to take a picture using your Android phone Camera .36
        Using the Gallery Icon...43
        Setting up a Gmail Account 44
        How to Sign out...52
Customizing your mail **54**
    How to open the Gmail Settings 54
        How to add a contact...56

How to import your contacts and Mail 60

How to Back up your Android Phone................................. 61

How to share files with your friends using your Android phone... 62

Accessing your Quick Settings 67

How to find your lost Android Phone 69

What does find My Device entails? 74

How to find your Android Phone with the 'Find My Device app.' 78

Frequently asked questions of Android Users............ 82

The major setbacks of Android phones.............................. 90

Conclusion 91

INTRODUCTION

When you buy a new Android phone or you are moving from an iPhone to an Android device can be a little problematic and thus might take a little while for you to get used to how things work on an Android. You might not get the authentic Android experience as Google intended, and you won't see the same messaging unification across devices all at once. Still, looking at the bright side, you will no longer be restricted to things like in-app restrictions. You will have purchasing freedom like never before. You even get to transfer files between you and your friends without restriction, unlike you might have experienced in your previous phone.

If you are jumping onto the Android bandwagon for the first time, there's a lot for you to figure out. This is why I have written this book; in it, I have put together everything you need to scale through on using an Android phone and its numerous functions. This is a comprehensive guide on how to use each of the platforms on your Android Phone.

In this book, you will learn how to use your Android Phone in general; this book is going to be basically for beginners, for people who have never really used Android or who are very unfamiliar with it, so I'm going to go through some basic stuff in this book. So if you know much about Android at all, then see, this book will probably not be of much help to you. I'm just going to focus on fundamental things to get people going who don't know anything about Android, so there are a few things I want to talk about before we get into the natural kinds of stuff.

GETTING STARTED

Navigating on an Android device

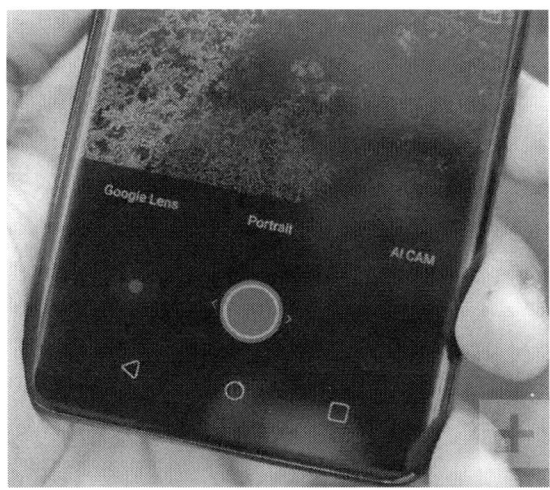

On a typical android, there are four buttons that you must have, include:

- ➢ You must have a home button. (which is the circle in the middle of the Phone above)

> It would help if you had a menu button, and most time, it doesn't say menu anymore.

> There is a back button. (which is the one on the left-hand side of the home button in the Phone above)

> There is a search button.

These four buttons are the ones that you see most of the time on Android: home, menu, back, and search, sometimes this can be taken down to just three, but usually, you will see these four, and they are never in this order it is never home menu back search sometimes they've all switched around, it just depends on which Phone you have.

It is still possible for you to bring back the three-button navigation system if that pleases you. Here's how:

1. Swipe down from the top of your screen to expand your Notification panel, then tap the gear icon.

2. Tap System and then tap Gestures.

3. Tap System Navigation.

4. Tap the circle located next to the 3-Button Navigation.

Most manufacturers typically equip their Android devices with the three-button navigation system at the bottom and then use additional gesture controls. Let's look at what each button is capable of doing in detail.

The back button, which is located on the left, will take you back to the last thing you did in an app, and it can also take you to the previous page open in your mobile browser.

Tap and hold the button down when using your browser and it will also automatically open up a menu that will gives you easy access to your favorite bookmarks, browsing history, and the websites you visit most often.

The button resides on the right side for Samsung phones, and you can move it to the left in your settings.

- Go to settings
- Go to display
- Go to the Navigation bar of your Android phone and click on edit

Home button

The Home button is located in the middle, and it will simply take you back to your home screen. In the most recent version of Android, holding down the home button will activate your Google Assistant.

Above is the home screen of a typical Android phone. Each Phone has a screen like this. The home screen is where it will take you each time you click on the home button. The look of your home screen depends on how the manufacturer of the Phone designed it, but you can also make some adjustments to it.

How to change the look of your home screen

To change the look of your home screen, tap and hold down the home button. It will now give you room to set your screen to your liking.

Overview button

Tapping the Overview button gives you a vertical list of every open and active app on your mobile device. This allows you to navigate between various apps by just tapping on your screen. Double tapping the overview button enables you to jump straight back into the app you used last.

This button resides on the left side of Samsung phones, and you can move it to the right:

- ➢ Go to settings
- ➢ Go to display
- ➢ Go to the Navigation bar and click on edit

Finally, some phones have gesture navigation enabled by default, and this eliminates all on-screen navigation controls.

The good thing about most Androids is that you are not limited to their way of doing things. You can easily change things to suit your preference. In most Androids, there is usually room to edit your input experience regardless of the manufacturer.

If you are trying to figure out how to use your phone and you need to find something that focuses on a particular phone of your choice that will likely be a waste of your precious time. If you are still a beginner, all you need to do is to learn the basics. Because every Android Phone has little quirks to it that are different from other ones, so once you get the basic general idea of how Android works, you need to find something that talks specifically about your Phone to help you out. But generally, you are going to have the four buttons as mentioned above; sometimes, the buttons are hard buttons when they're built onto the case, while sometimes, they are soft when they are on the screen. So, if your screen is off, you don't see those buttons. You only see it when the screen comes on, and then you can push those buttons called on-screen navigation.

So, depending on the app you are in, some of the buttons will do different things, like the menu will do something different depending on what app you have open. If you have Facebook available and push the menu, it will open up one type of menu. Another example is if you are in your phone dialer where you can call people. You move the menu, and you are going to get a different-looking menu. The same thing applies for the search button, depending on where you are on your Phone, whatever place you are at, the search button is going to bring up something different, and the home button is always going to take you back to your home screen and back is going to go to the screen before that.

So now another fundamental thing I want to talk about for Android is that the term Android refers to the operating system; when Verizon first came out with their androids, they called them droids, and that was more of a way to designate the actual Phone, and it was to enhance recognition. Still, it also created confusion because Android, as you already know, is an operating system, while Verizon's phones were called droids. Android is just like you have Windows operating systems on your desktop computer. You may have Windows XP, or you may have Windows 7 or Windows 8. All those are just different versions of the Windows operating system, and that's what Android is but for phones and tablets. It is what lets you turn your Phone on to make calls, open up Facebook, and open any stuff; that's what the operating system does.

Android has lots of different versions, and what Android did very early on is they started referring to their versions as desert names the A and B, and this goes in alphabetical order the a and the B I never believe had a desert name; they just went by alpha and beta. Starting at C, they started calling them by desert names. So, C was a cupcake, D was a donut, E was Éclair, f was Froyo or frozen yogurt, G was gingerbread, H was honeycomb, I was Ice Cream Sandwich, J was a jelly bean, and K is KitKat. The list goes on and on, and they were released in alphabetical order. Android phones all have an Android operating system running on them, but each Android Phone has a specific Android operating system working in it.

Android originally was an operating system for phones developed by a company that Google did not own, and different people created it. Google eventually bought the Android operating system, and now Android is Google's phone mobile operating system, so when you are running Android, you are running something that is developed by the Google company, given that you need to have a Google Gmail account to enable you to utilize your Android Phone to the fullest. This is because the Google Gmail account works faster on an Android phone since they are both made by the same company. I know some of you may have old hot mail accounts or yahoo accounts or, you know, some other, something like that, but to use these to their fullest potential, you need to have a Gmail account.

How you can set up your new Phone.

Before you can do anything on your Android Phone, you need to switch the Phone on and set it up. Join me as I go over the things you should do after turning on your screen.

The first thing you will see is your Welcome screen, after which you are to follow the following steps:

1. Select your preferred language, then tap Start.

2. Connect to a mobile network by inserting the SIM card if you have not done that already.

3. Connect to a local wireless network by tapping on your network and entering the network password.

4. You can now set up the device as a new phone or choose to copy apps and data from an older machine. If you wish to duplicate apps and data, there are three methods by which you can do that:

    ➤ Connect the older Phone using a USB cable.
    ➤ Connect to your backup stored in Google Drive.
    ➤ Transfer your data from an iPhone. If you wish to transfer your data from an iPhone, go to android.com/switch and follow the instructions on the website.

5. Sign in to your Google Account. If you don't have one, then tap 'Get an Account' and follow the instructions. You don't need a Google account to use your Phone, but it is a requirement to download apps, back up your data, or use Google apps and services.

6. If you're using a cloud backup, select your service from the list if there is more than one service listed. You may be asked to enter the Pin associated with your backup.

7. Select the list of things you want to restore; they may include: Apps, Contacts, SMS Messaging, Device Settings, or Call History.

8. Set the appropriate date and time.

9. Click on 'I Agree' when asked for the Google Services and the legal terms.

10. Set up your Screen Lock using a PIN, pattern, or password. This is like a plan b, whenever your Android Phone fails to read your fingerprint or when it fails to capture your facial details correctly.

11. Set up the fingerprint scanner or Face ID; you can also choose to set both. To set up your fingerprint scanner, place your preferred finger on the fingerprint sensor so that it can capture your fingerprint pattern. If you are unsure how to do this, do not worry, your Android will work you through the process.

12. Set up your Google Assistant. This is artificial intelligence that acts like your friend, you can ask it questions, and it will quickly look them up on the internet and supply you with answers. It makes your Android phone usage seamless.

Google Assistant integration

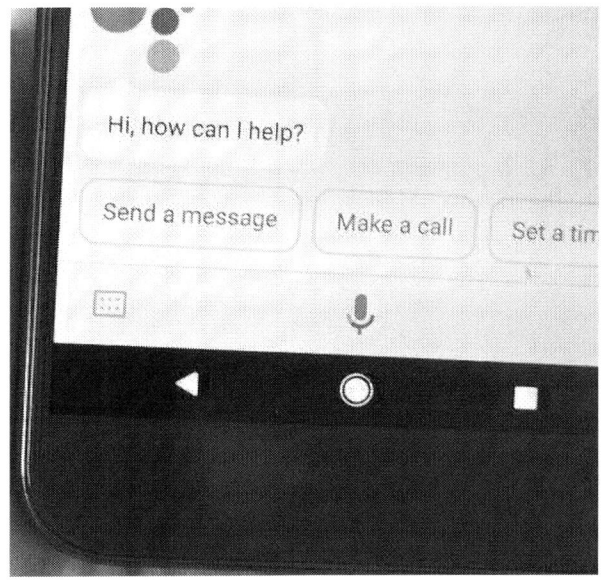

Google Assistant is available on all Android devices running on Marshmallow 6.0 or later, and it has one significant advantage over other mobile operating systems.

In terms of the search engine, the Google assistant is an even more reliable partner than 'Siri,' the iPhone assistant.

For example, Google Assistant uses your search history to display news and stories relevant to what you like or what you love to update. The same applies to the football news and live soccer updates. It also analyzes your travel habits and brings up relevant information while providing you with a time estimate for the duration of your journey and the best/shortest route to take.

To access your Google Assistant, long-press the Home button. You can also activate it using your voice, say "Hey Google," using voice commands, and it will immediately respond to you. If the voice command and long pressing home button don't work, go to the Google app on your Android Phone to change the settings for accessing it and change it to suit your preference.

1. Set up your Google Play. This is used to make payments online. This way, you won't be asked for too many details every time you complete a transaction.

Google Pay

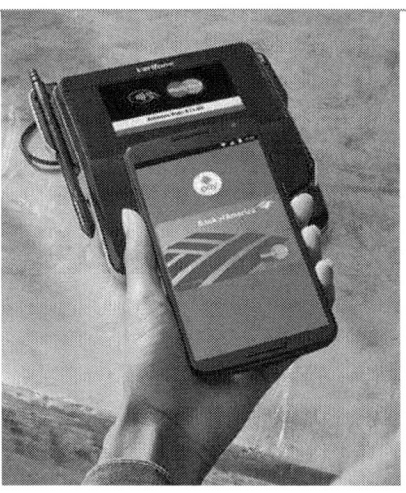

Google Pay is an even more exciting feature, just as mentioned above. It is available on all Android devices that run on the Android version 8.0 and above and is a significant advantage over other operating systems, which is the fact that it enables you to make payments from anywhere in the world without going through too many rigorous processes since it already has your details stored in it. It allows you to store physical gift cards, and pay for items in-store, and even more.

- ➤ Google Pay comes preloaded on many devices, but it is not a cause for alarm if you don't have it in yours. Just go over to your Google play store and download it.

- ➤ If you already have a card in your Google Account, then confirm the details to add it to Google Play. You can also add a new card from any bank allowed, take a picture of your card and confirm the details.

Google Play

One of the essential things on your Phone is the Play Store because the Play Store is where you can go and download different apps, it is where you are going to go to critical social media apps like Facebook if you don't have that as an app, it is where you are going to go and get angry birds as a game for you to play it or for your kids to play. So, when you want to use the Google play store, here are the simple steps you must follow; bear in mind that you must have an account to access these steps.

- ➤ When you click on the Google Play store with your Android Phone, it will ask you to add your Google account. Do not forget that your Google account is the account that you created earlier on.

> Tap existing instead of new because you already have one.

> Type in your username and password; once you have done that, click on 'sign in .' It will let you open up your Google account to get the Google play store.

So, you just added Play Store; remember it is essential that you set up your account because that is the only way you can access the Google Play store where you will get all your different apps and stuff.

After setting up your device, the next thing to do is check for software updates; usually, your Phone will automatically search for updates once you connect to a network service.

If your Phone does not automatically search for updates when connected to a network service, you can follow these few steps to do it yourself.

> Swipe down from to top to expand the notification panel and tap the gear icon.

> Tap System.

> Tap Advanced.

> Tap System Update.

> Tap Check for Update.

You can now sit back and watch your Android as it checks to see if any updates are available. If there are available updates, you can download and install them.

The Notification Panel

When you swipe down from the top of your screen, you will see the Notification Shade. The notification shade is where most activities are recorded, and apps broadcast their notifications in a row. At the top of the panel, you will find the Quick Settings bar, which you can also expand by dragging down its "handle."

In Android phones, there is usually an option to dismiss all notifications on the panel. You will also see an opportunity to manage the messages. You can use the manage option to choose how you want your notices to be arranged. When you are done with the notification panel, tap on the home button to dismiss the notification panel.

Android Phones User Guide for Beginners

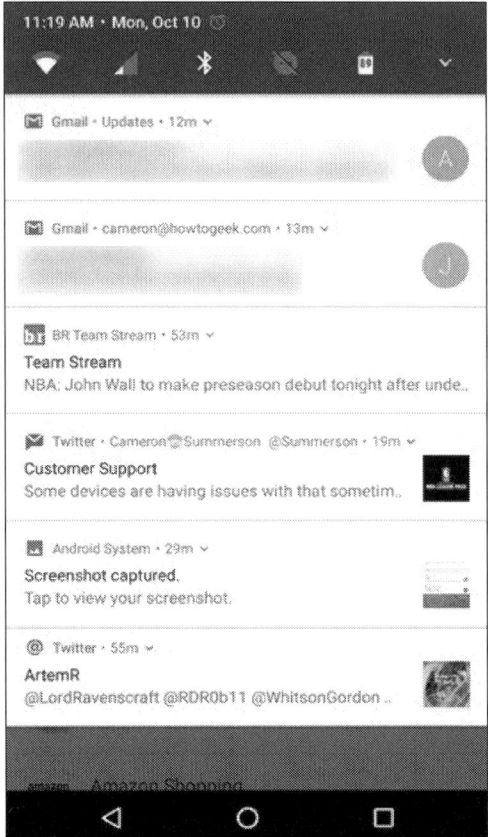

The Status Bar

At the top of your Phone is the status bar, just as you can see in the picture below. It never leaves the display, except in few cases like watching a movie or playing a game. The status bar displays information like the time, network speed, battery percentage, and notifications. All Android phones have the status bar in the joint because it is ever-present in all Android phones.

How to Send a Text Message on Your Android Phone

You can use your Android Phone to send text messages to other phone users, regardless of the type of Phone they use. The one and only requirement is that you must have a registered phone number, and the person you are sending to must have a registered phone number.

Sending a text message is one of the easiest things to do with your Android Phone. Let us go through the steps involved in sending a text message:

1. Open your phone message app, and you will see a list of current conversations which are blank because you are yet to have one, and they are all organized by contact name or phone number.

2. Locate the name of the person you want to send the message to. If you don't have the person's name saved on your contact, you will have to type in the person's phone number. You can add multiple recipients for your message by either marking the contacts or typing in the names.

3. Type your text message. The picture below is an example of what a text message conversation looks like.

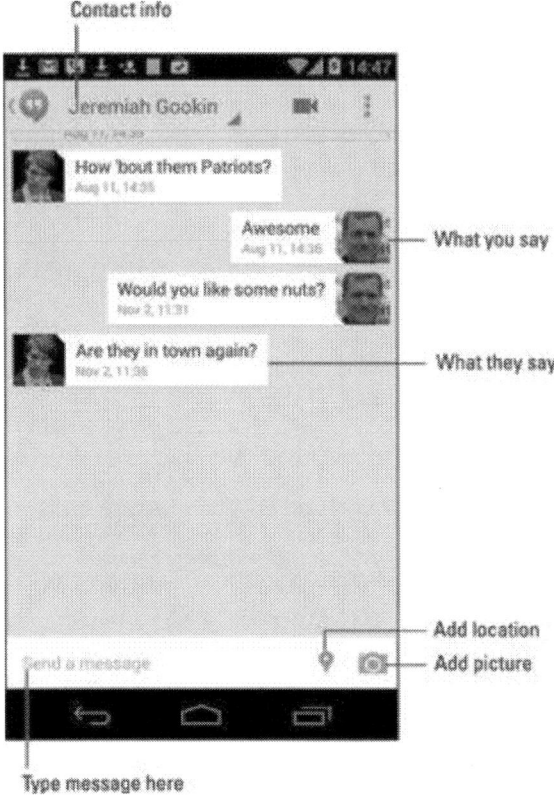

4. Touch the send icon as shown below to send your message.

You can also send a text message to a number directly from your contact list without copying the number. Just click on the 'more' option of the contact and tap the text messaging icon there. After you touch the icon, the Phone's text messaging app starts, and you can compose your message.

Note:

- You can only send text messages to a mobile phone; you cannot send to a landline.

- You can send a single text message to as many recipients as you want. You have to add all of them, as explained earlier.

- When you receive a group message, the choice remains yours to reply to them all or reply to an individual. Look for an answer-all button that will appear while you are composing your response.

- The messaging app saves your conversation so that you can continue an exchange at any time. You can also look up any talk to remind yourself of what has been said.

Remember, for your safety, do not text and drive.

How to Make and Receive Calls on an Android Phone

Mobile phones have gone through various advancements since the introduction of the first mobile phone in 1980. Today smartphones have become more powerful than people thought they would. They even have an operating system like a computer called the "Android Operating system." The smartphone you have is capable of placing calls to different regions and different countries of the world.

Let's go through how to place a call using your Android Phone.

There are four methods for making phone calls on your Android Phone

There are several ways to place a phone call on your Android Phone, the only thing all the methods in the joint are that they all start the same way, which is to power your phone and goes to your home screen and tap the phone app.

After successfully powering your Phone, you can use any phone app on your Android Phone to place a call.

1. To place a call, use the dial pad, which looks like what is shown below, to place a call and enter the number you want to call.

Android Phones User Guide for Beginners

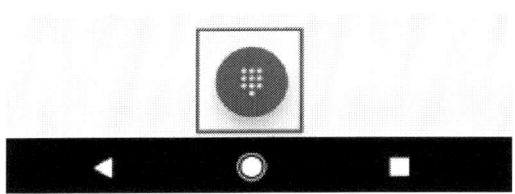

If you already have the number saved, you have to tap on the number and select to make a call.

When you tap on the dialer, the picture above is an example of what comes up next. Tap the digits on the keypad. If you make a mistake while typing in the number, use the 'X' button to delete the wrong one(s). After typing in the number, click on the green icon below the keypad to place your call.

2. **You can visit your call log to call someone who just called you:** This is a simple method of making a call to someone you previously called or who called you previously. To place the call.

   ➢ Tap the Call History tab

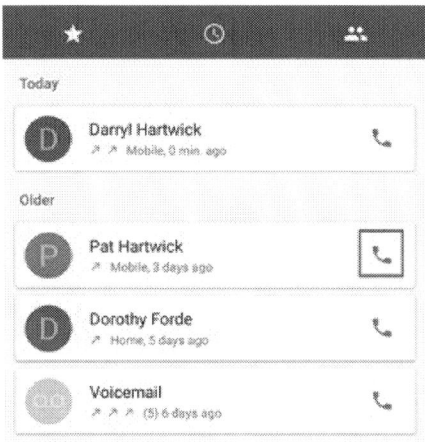

The call history tab shows you the dates and times of all the calls you have made for some time, and it also indicates who made the call.

   ➢ A green arrow indicates that you placed the call.

   ➢ A blue arrow indicates that you received the call.

   ➢ A red arrow indicates that you missed the person's call.

To place a call from the Call history tab, tap the call icon located beside the person's name.

Note:

You can block a person's number in the call history tab. To block a number:

- ➢ Tap and hold the person's number, and it will bring out a list of options for you.

- ➢ Scroll down, and you will see 'block contact.'

- ➢ Tap on 'block contact,' and the person will not be allowed to place a call to you again.

You can choose to unblock the contact whenever it pleases you.

3. **You can place a call to someone directly from your contact list:** Go to your contact list, tap the contacts tab at the top of the screen, as shown below.

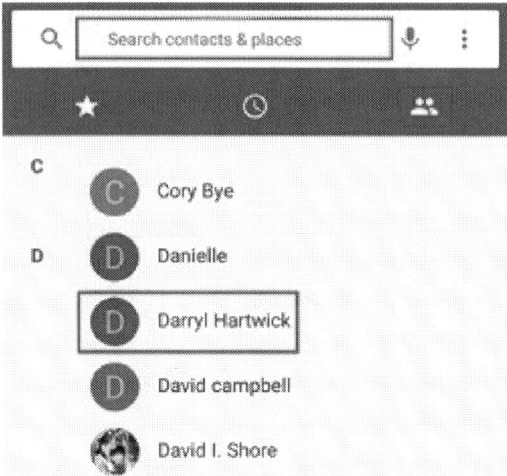

This contact tab shows you a list of all the people whose numbers you have saved on your Phone. The contacts are arranged in alphabetical order for accessible locations of contacts. If you have a large array of connections, then scrolling down will be a waste of time. Tap on the search icon at the top of your screen and type in the person's name or phone number to locate the person.

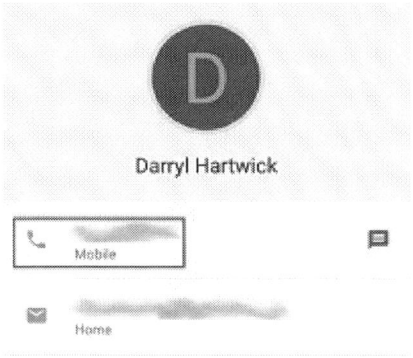

When you locate the phone number, tap their name. The picture above is an example of the screen shown on the next page. Tap on the call icon and place your call.

4. **You can set a number on your speed dial list:** This is an easy way to place a call to someone you contact frequently. All you need is a single tap, and you will play the call.

   ➢ Go to your contact information page, select the contact as a 'favorite.' This will automatically add them to your speed dial list.

   ➢ To do this, tap the 'Favorites' button, which is the star icon located in the top-right corner of your screen.

   ➢ The presence of a hollow star identifies a contact that is not located on your speed dial list yet, and the company of a solid star determines someone who has been added to your speed dial list.

   ➢ When you are done, then tap the Back arrow located in the top-left corner of the screen (as in the picture below) to go back to your contacts.

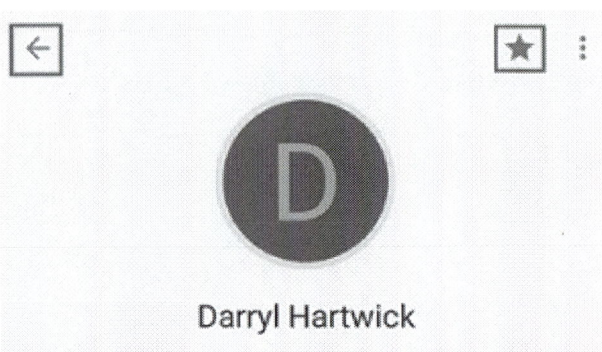

Tap the speed dial tab (located at the top of your screen). This shows a list of all the people who have been added to your speed dial list. You can call any one of them with a single tap.

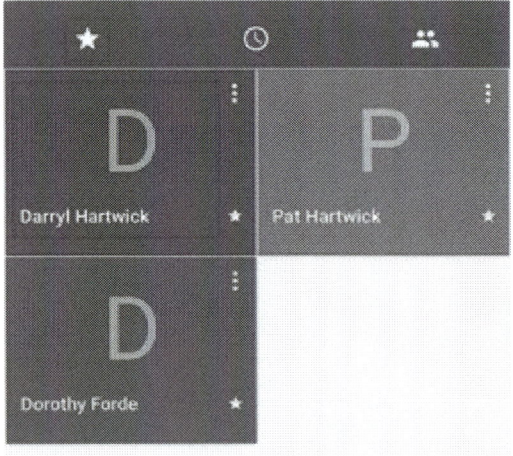

How you can receive a call on your Android Phone

When someone calls you on your Android Phone, you have different options of picking the call, and they depend on whether your Phone's screen is turned on or off.

If your Phone's screen lock is on:

This implies that it will show the caller's information at the top of your screen. At the same time, it will show a white and green call icon at the bottom of your screen.

Press and hold call icon, and:

> ➢ Move your finger towards the top of the screen to accept the call.

> ➢ Move your finger towards the bottom of the screen to decline the call.

The choice to accept or decline the call is yours to make.

Your Android Phone gives you the ability to reject a call and automatically send a text message to the caller to explain why you can't accept the ring at the moment.

To send an automatic message when a call is declined.

- Tap and hold your message button at the bottom of your screen, as indicated by the picture above, then move your finger towards the middle of the screen.

- It brings up a menu at the bottom of the screen containing a few common quick responses that can explain why you declined the call. Tap one of them, and it automatically sends the message to the caller.

- You can tap write your own at the bottom part of the screen, enabling you to create a unique message of your own.

```
Can't talk now. What's up?

I'll call you right back.

I'll call you later.

Can't talk now. Call me later?
```
```
Write your own...
```

If your screen lock is off:

You will see the caller's name or number at the top of your screen, alongside two buttons. Tap Answer to accept the call or tap to reject the call.

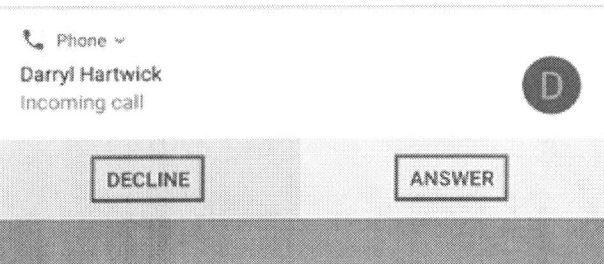

What you can do on an Android phone call

Once you have connected with someone on a call, there are several options available for you to use. Let us go through the options that are available to you in detail:

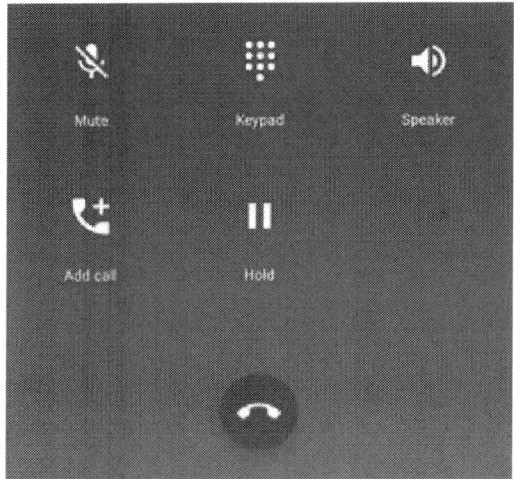

1. **Muting a call**

mute button, as shown in the picture above, turns your microphone off. This helps you pay more attention to what the other caller is saying, assuming your background noise interferes with your hearing. You can turn the microphone back on by tapping it.

2. Accessing your Keypad

Tapping this button will bring up your Phone's dial pad. This is mainly used when you are on a call with an automated system like your service provider, which requires you to input digits to make your choice. Tap the 'X' button located at the top-left corner of the dial pad to close it.

3. Speaker

Tapping this button switches you to a loudspeaker, assuming you were using an earpiece and you need others to hear the call. Or if you are not using an earpiece and you still need others to listen to the ring. Tapping the button again switches it back to the normal mode it was in.

4. Adding a Call

If you want to connect another person to your current call, then tap this button, or if you wish to place a call to another person while your recent call is on. Tapping this button allows you to set the call to the person while keeping your current call on Hold. This has some similarities to a conference call, and it all depends on your service provider.

5. Putting a call on Hold

This button, when tapped, will temporarily pause your current call without hanging up on the caller. Tapping the button again will resume the call.

6. Ending a Call

Tapping the red button at the bottom of your screen will automatically disconnect the call.

How to save a contact on your Android phone

1. Go to your dialer

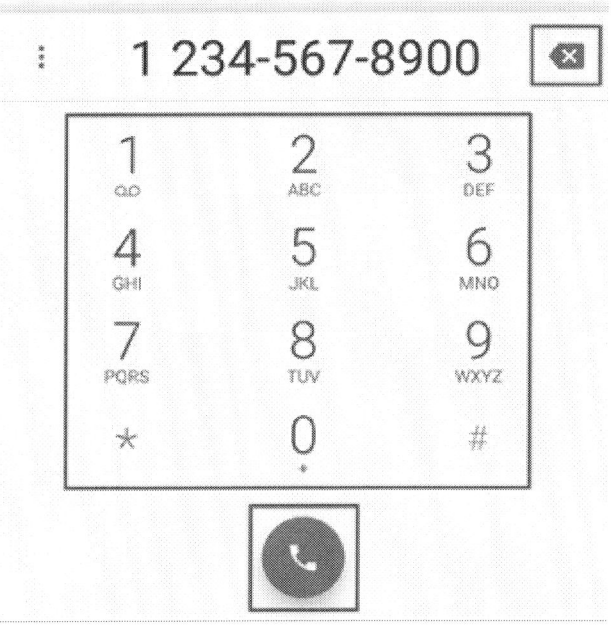

2. Type in the dialer, the phone number you wish to save.
3. After typing in the number, you will see an option for you to either 'create a new contact' or 'add to a contact' or 'send SMS'

4. Click on 'Create new contact'
5. In the next page, put in the name you will like to save the person's name with. You should use something with which you can easily remember the person.
6. After putting in the name, click on the arrow sign for good, and with that you have successfully saved a contact.

How to take a picture using your Android phone Camera

The Android phone camera keeps getting better with each new version of the Android operating system. With your camera, you can take pictures, view pictures, edit pictures and share them with friends and families. In this section, I will show you how to use your Android phone camera in few steps:

1. Locate the camera app on your phone, which is labelled 'camera'

2. There is an option to switch between the front camera of your phone and the back camera, depending on how you want it. To switch between both, tap any of the icons as shown below.

3. Your Android phone camera has different features, such as filters, stickers and many other effects. To use any of these effects, tap the 'effects' icon.

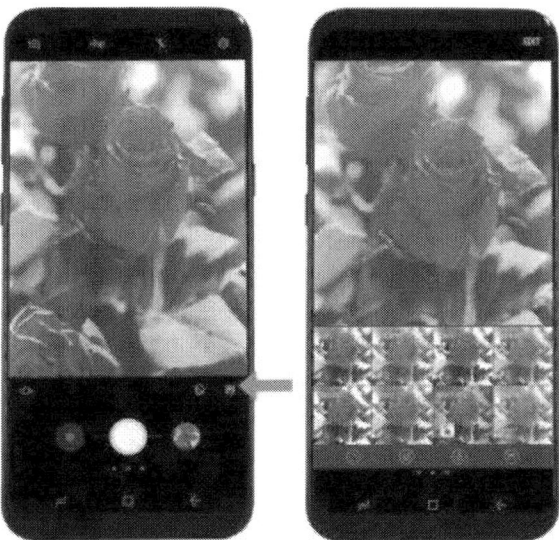

4. To focus your camera, touch the area of the screen you will like to focus on. A circle like in the picture below will appear on your screen, and the camera will automatically focus on that spot.

5. You can "Zoom in" or "Zoom out" when taking a picture.
   - To zoom in: Place your two fingers on your screen and drag them towards each other.
   - To zoom out: Place your two fingers on your screen and drag them apart.

6. To take the photo, press the shutter button as indicated on the picture below.

Note:

You can take a screenshot of your screen, this captures all the things you currently have on your screen. Taking a screenshot of your screen can be done using various means, depending on your Android phone settings. But a particular method is peculiar to all Android phone versions, to do this:

- Press and hold your 'Power button' and 'Volume down button' simultaneously.

Using the Gallery Icon

The gallery is where all your photos are kept. To access the gallery, tap the Gallery icon as shown in the picture below.

Setting up a Gmail Account

Since you should have a Gmail account to use your Android better, let me walk you through creating a Gmail account. You do not have to pay to get one done for you, so long as you have your Android Phone and a good internet connection.

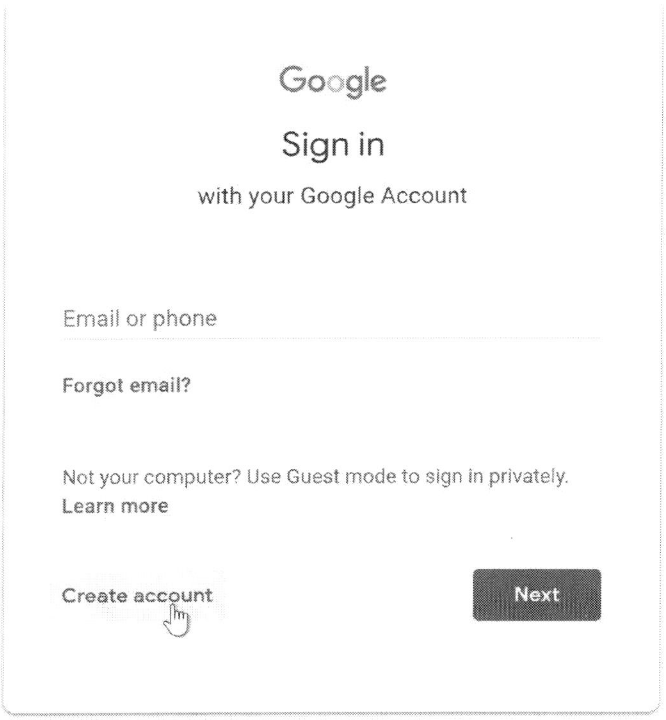

> Google
>
> Sign in
>
> with your Google Account
>
> Email or phone
>
> Forgot email?
>
> Not your computer? Use Guest mode to sign in privately. Learn more
>
> Create account   Next

1. Go to your phone web browser, and in the search button, click on Gmail.com. There will be a button for login and one for creating an account. As you click on create an account, it will bring up where you can create a free Google Gmail account.

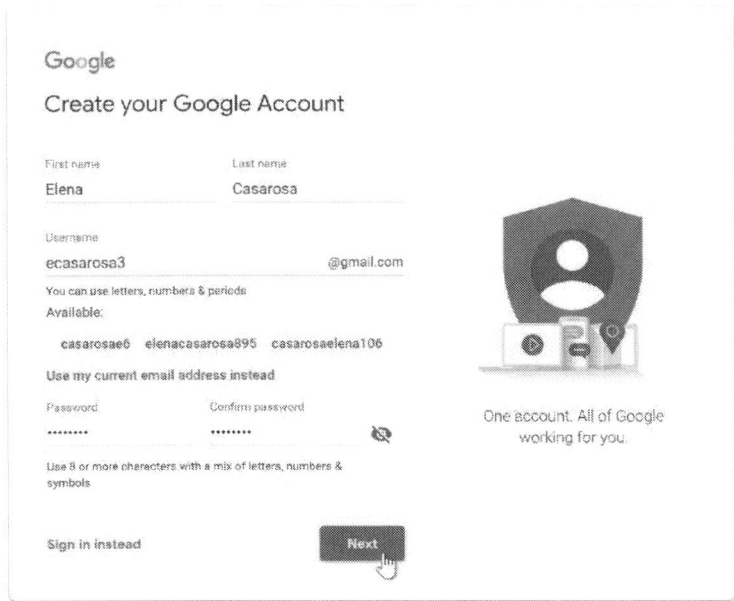

2. So, you will have to fill in all the details, just as in the picture above. You will want to choose your username but bear in mind that many people have usernames, so if you were to put your name, there is no doubt that you would have used someone else. You will have to develop a unique username for you alone, one that's going to be different from what anybody else has.

Android Phones User Guide for Beginners

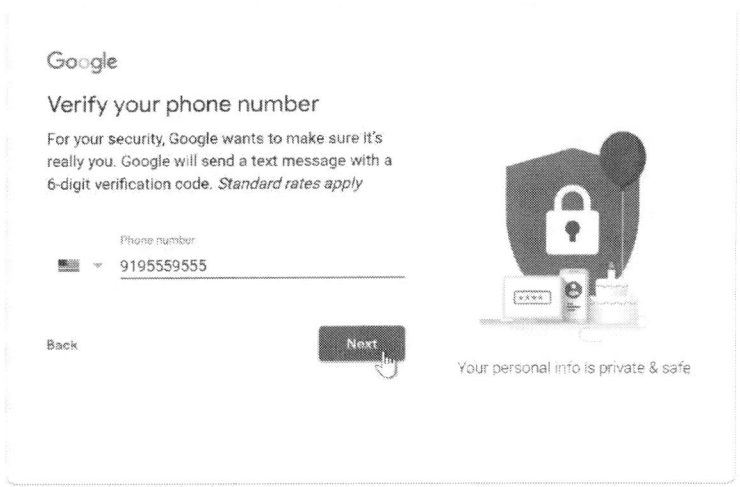

3. After filling in your details, proceed to the next page, where you will have to put in a phone number that will serve as your recovery phone number. A recovery phone number helps you in situations where you forget your password and lose access to your account. With it, you can send a new password to you, and you can reclaim ownership of your account.

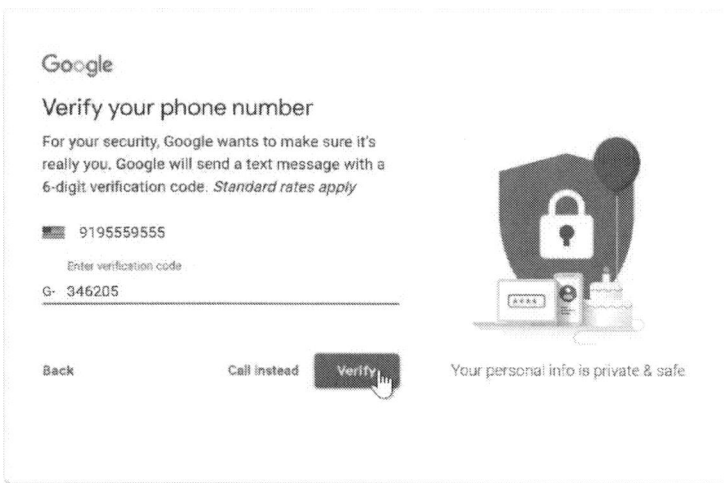

4. Ensure you use a functioning phone number because you will receive a verification code from Google, with which you can complete your steps.

Android Phones User Guide for Beginners

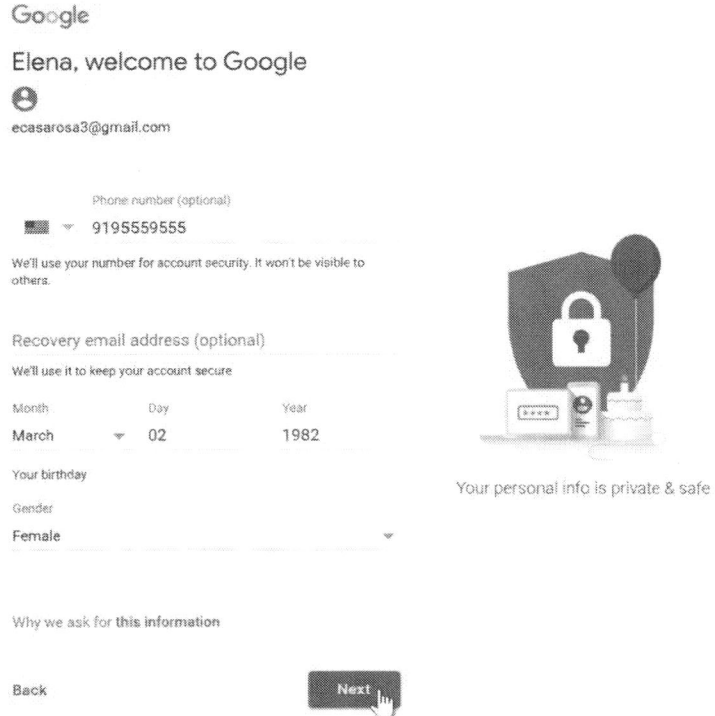

5. On the next page, you will see a form where you will fill in your personal information, like your name, your gender, and your birthday. This helps Google keep track of their users and celebrate with you on important days like your birthday.

6. The picture above is what you will see on your next page. If you have the liberty of time, you can go through the policy, but if you don't, you can click on 'I agree' the whole idea of the policy is to favor you, so fear not. With this, your account is created and now fully functional.

After creating your account, you can now use the Gmail app on your android device. Once you open the Gmail app, you have to fill in your details, and it will be connected. It is giving you access to your emails at your fingertips.

If you decide to check your mail on your friend's Android phone or in a web browser, you will have to sign in. You can do that in just a few steps:

Android Phones User Guide for Beginners

1. Go to the website; www.gmail.com

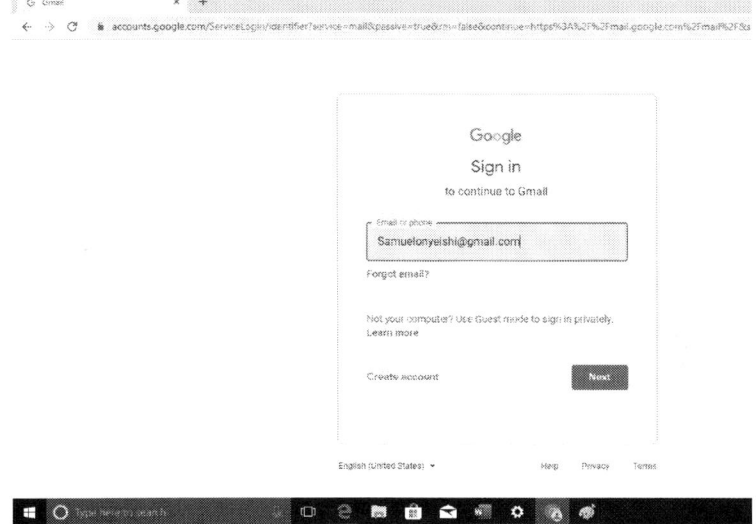

2. Type your username in the space provided and click on next to move on.

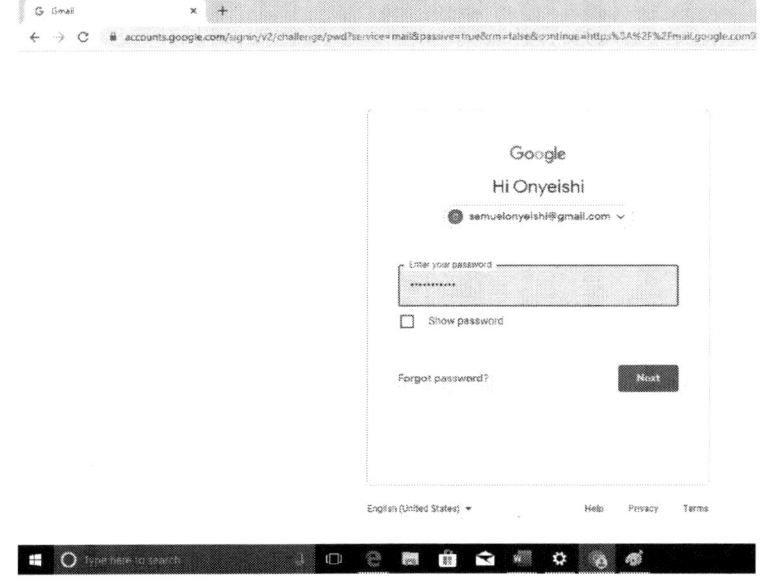

3. On the next page, as you can see above, type in your password. With that, you will be logged in successfully.

If you ever forget your password, you can click on the forgot password option. You can follow the following steps to get a new password.

How to Sign out

Whenever you use a friend's phone or a public computer to check your mail, always endeavor to sign out to safeguard your privacy. Signing out is very easy:

1. Click on the circular icon with your initials in it, and it is located at the upper right-hand part.

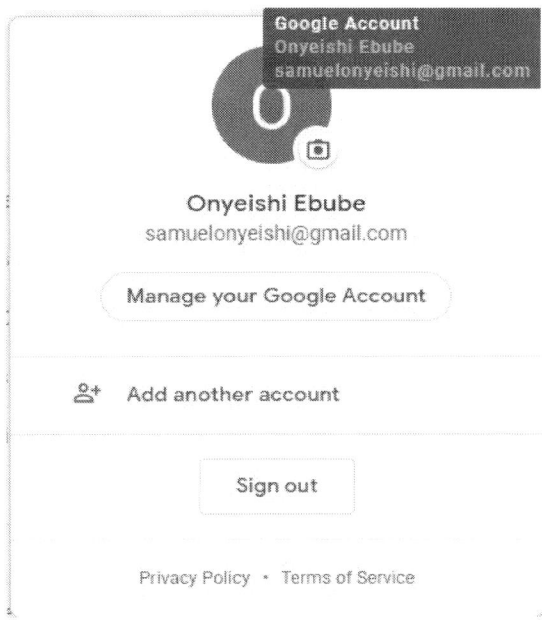

2. The picture above is what comes up when you click on the icon containing your initials. Click on the sign-out, and it will sign you out.

You need a Gmail account to use your Android Phone to the fullest of its potentials. Most people, who used phones with other operating systems before the Android operating system, like windows intelligent phones on the windows mobile platform, might have used different forms of mail like Hotmail. Those who used Hotmail as their primary email account can transfer all their correspondence to the new Gmail account. Goggle currently gives over 15 gigabytes of free storage with each Gmail account you have, which is quite generous.

CUSTOMIZING YOUR MAIL

You may want to make several adjustments to how your Gmail is looking and behaving for better usage. This is more than possible using the Gmail settings. The things you can do in the Gmail settings include:

- Setting an automatic reply system.

- Changing the theme of your Gmail account.

- Developing a list of auto-responses that you can choose from when replying to messages on your Gmail account.

How to open the Gmail Settings

These settings work for both your Gmail app and your Web browser Gmail, whichever you want to change.

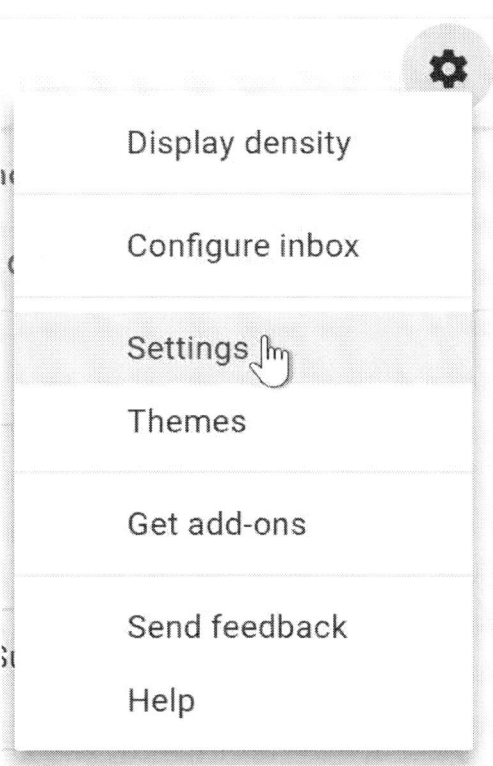

1. Look for the location of the gear icon. In most Android phones, and it will write settings on it to make locating it more straightforward.

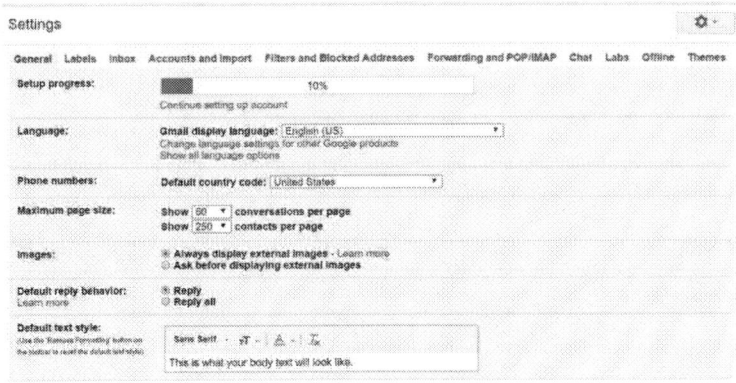

2. On the next page that opens, you adjust things to suit your preference. Ensure you save your changes when you are done. Then exit the settings area, and it would have made all your changes.

How to add a contact

Like all the major email providers, Gmail lets you keep an address book of your contact, and this means you don't have to memorize every one of your friend's email addresses. You can also add other contact information, like their phone numbers, birthdays, and physical addresses.

To add a contact, follow these steps:

1. Click on the 'Google apps' button.

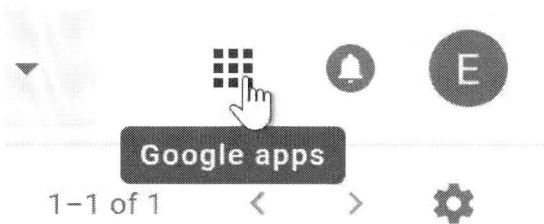

2. Click on the Contacts button located in the drop-down menu.

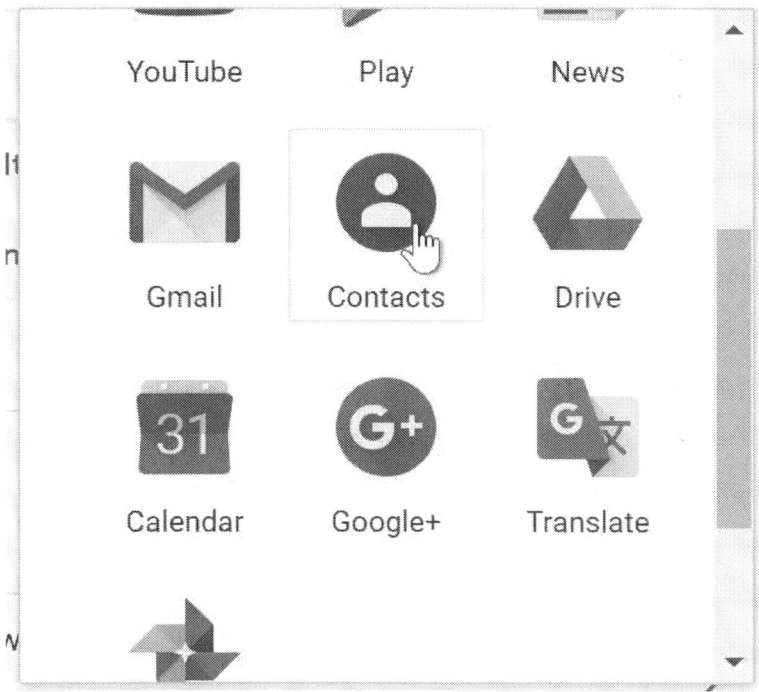

3. Your contacts screen will appear. Click on the Add new contact button located in the right corner of the lower part of your screen.

4. Enter the contact information, and then click Save.

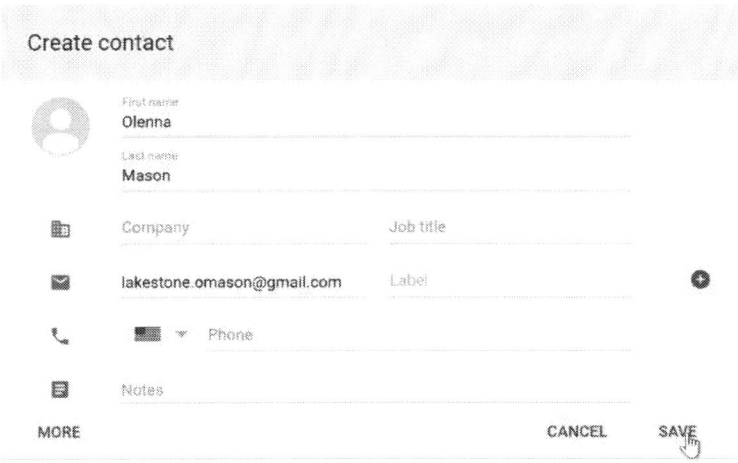

To edit a contact which you have added, you will have to follow these few steps:

1. In the drop-down menu of your 'Google app, ' select Contacts.

Android Phones User Guide for Beginners

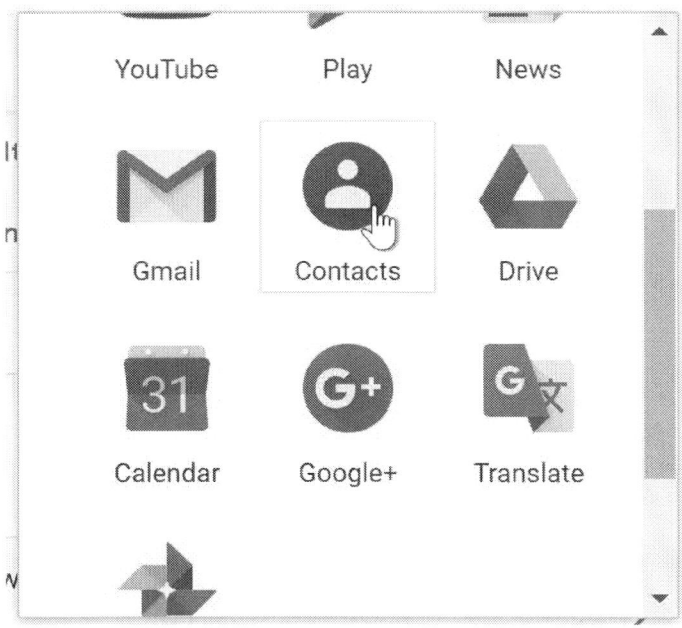

2. Locate the contact you want to edit, and click 'Edit Contact.'

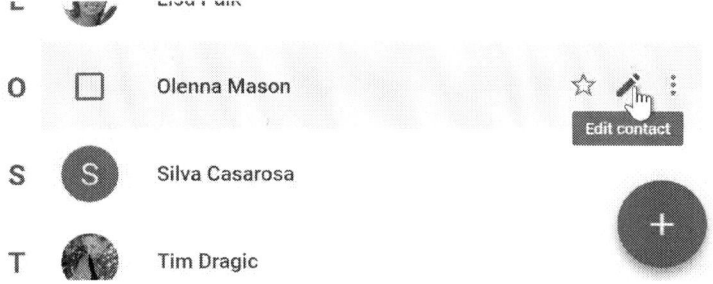

3. You can as well make any other changes you will like to make.

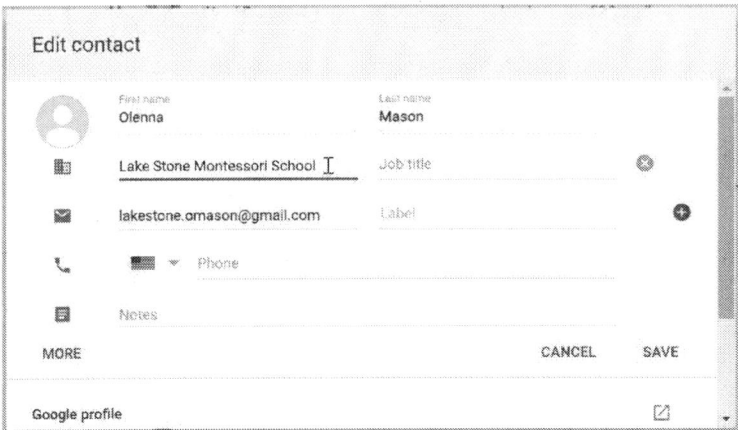

Gmail is created to automatically add people's addresses to your contact when you send them a mail. It is left for you to go over to the edit section and edit the person's details as you see fit.

How to import your contacts and Mail

You may already have a contact list from another email address, and it will be a lot of work to re-enter all of the information contained in it manually. Gmail saves you the stress and allows you to import your contacts from another email account. You can as well import all of your email messages from that account. Gmail supports importation from several email providers, including:

- Yahoo

- Hotmail

How to add contacts

1. Click the gear icon we talked about earlier located in the top-right corner of the page and select settings.

2. Go to 'Accounts' and click on 'Add a mail account.' You can follow the on-screen instructions for the easy importation of your Mail.

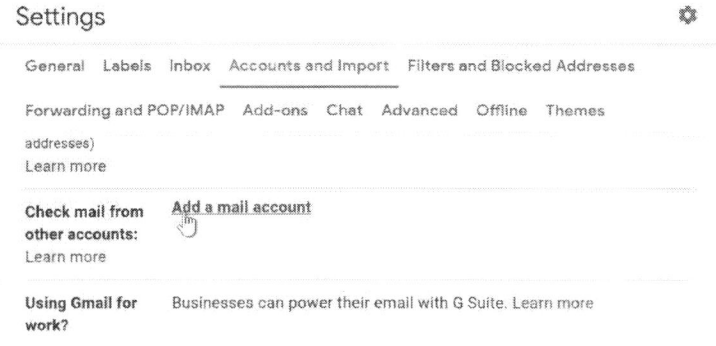

How to Back up your Android Phone

When you have gone through most of the steps, an essential thing which you must not forget to do is to back up your Phone. It is as crucial as breathing because you could lose everything you have on your Phone in less than an instant. So, you must make backing up your files to Google Drive a habit, that way, you will have nothing to fear even if your Phone gets stolen.

Here are the steps involved in backing up your Phone:

1. Swipe down from the top to expand your Notification panel and then tap the gear icon.

2. Tap System.

3. Tap Backup.

Note:

- ➢ Make sure you have turned on 'Back Up to Google Drive
- ➢ To back up your photos and videos to your google drive, you will have to use Google photos, which is a different process.

How to share files with your friends using your Android phone

The era of Bluetooth file transfer is long gone, now you can share more bulky files at an even faster rate using your Android phone. This can be done using the 'Xender application'. The Xender application shares files using Wi-Fi connection, it does not require an internet connection. The only condition is that both phones must have the Xender application installed and are in close range. To use the Xender app to share files is very easy, and I will explain how to do that in few steps:

If you do not have the Xender app installed on your phone, then go to your play store as explained in one of the aforementioned section.

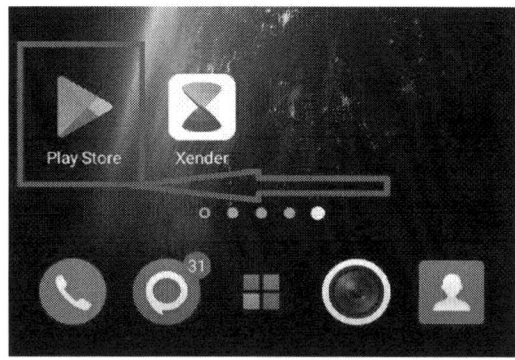

1. Search out the "Xender app" and install it.

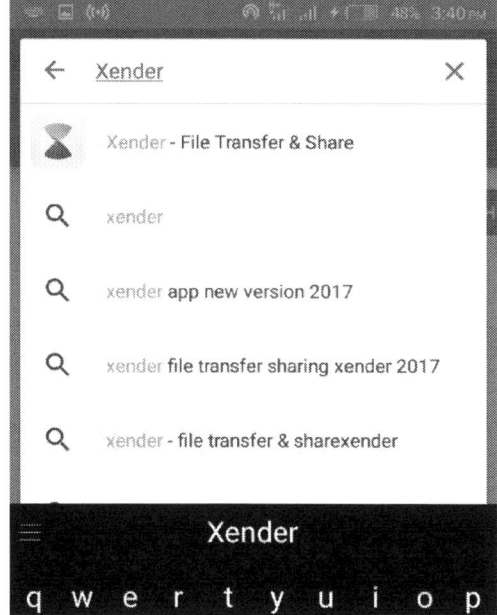

Launch the "Xender app" on both phones. You can do this just by tapping on the app, then wait for it to load.

To share a file: Select the file or app from your lists and click on 'Send' as seen in the picture below. Then the person you are sending to will have to click on 'Receive'. Your phone automatically creates a QR code which the receiver must scan to get connected.

Android Phones User Guide for Beginners

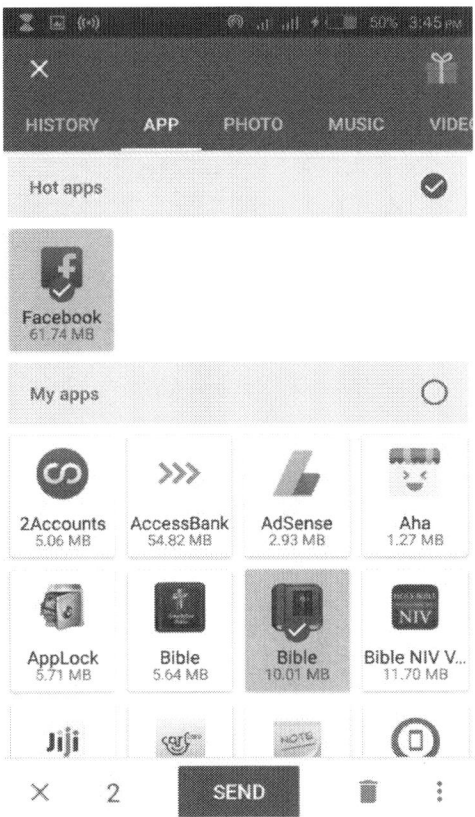

To receive a file: Scan the QR code and the connection will be initiated. The file automatically gets sent to you, provided you have the required space.

Setting up Multiple Screens

An Android phone gives you room to toggle through multiple screens. With earlier versions of Android, you could toggle through five screens, but you can toggle through as many screens as you want with the more advanced versions of our time.

As an Android phone user, you can now create shortcuts, group apps together in a folder, and even change your screen wallpaper. All this applies to widgets, too, so you are unlimited in what you can do. To access these tools, you have to tap on the screen and hold it for up to five seconds.

There is also something called the App Drawer, through which you can access all your apps. In most Android phones, it is usually out of sight and is located at the bottom of any screen.

Accessing your Quick Settings

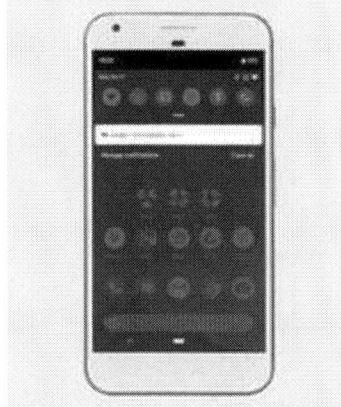

The Quick Settings bar is the easiest way for you to access all your mainly used features, and it usually has the same experience across all Android phones. It is one of the essential aspects of Android phones, and it can also be said to be the most used aspect. Each time a new version of Android is released, it is constantly updated. Accessing this bar without expanding the Notification panel can simply be done by swiping down from the top of your screen using two of your fingers. When you fully develop your Quick Settings panel, it is usually full of buttons that can span one or more pages. You can swipe to the left of your screen to navigate through the different pages. You will find out that the buttons are very easy to use.

- To turn on/off a feature like Bluetooth, you just have to tap the icon once.
- If you wish to access the function's settings, like accessing Bluetooth or Wi-Fi settings, press the button until the respective panel appears. This saves you time by giving you direct access to those settings versus tapping through various categories.

The Quick Settings bar also provides a slider for dimming and brightening the screen. Samsung phones have an additional toggle to turn on Outdoor Mode that illuminates the screen to its maximum for over 15 minutes.

Types of apps you should have

The choice of apps to have is left to you, but from my experience with most users, I can suggest a few essential apps which you should have as an Android phone user. They include:

- **Social apps include** Facebook, Instagram, WhatsApp, etc.
- **Apps for Shopping:** Walmart, Amazon, etc.
- **Apps for watching/streaming videos include** a VLC media player, MX player, Netflix, etc.
- **Apps for playing/streaming Music include** Audiomack, Boomplay, Spotify, etc.

- **Apps for your work have** Zoom app, Microsoft Office, Adobe packages, etc.

If you are a fan of games, then I have a few apps for streaming game consoles to your Android phones. Companies like Microsoft and Sony provide these apps so that people can stream their game consoles directly to their Android phones. They include:

- Playstation app
- Xbox family settings
- Xbox Game pass
- PS remote play
- Xbox Game streaming
- PS4 second screen

How to find your lost Android Phone

Losing your Phone is solely the worst. Not having the ability to answer calls or text messages is frustrating, and it's particularly terrible if you've ultimately got no plan wherever your Phone may be. There's additionally a risk to your privacy, as somebody who picks it up may be able to get into it and access your info. If your Android Phone is presently lost or taken, then this section of this book is for you. In this section, I will show you ways to assist in getting back your lost Phone.

I will be showing you two different, straightforward ways in which you can find your Android Phone if you've lost it or if someone took it. Each one you decide to try out works well, and therefore the 1st technique doesn't even need you to install an app on your Phone before you misplaced it. In the end, I will additionally tell you about four friendly apps you must install on your Android Phone to assist you in case you ever misplace your Android. Let's delve into the various techniques for finding your Phone.

Making use of Google

Simply looking "find my Android" with Google Search will get you started towards finding your lost Android Phone. When you log into your Google account on your Device, Google will assist you in finding it, and this is another reason you should create a Google account using the steps explained earlier. Here's how to find your Phone using Google

> ➢ Visit Google.com in your preferred web browser

On your laptop or a friend's mobile device, open your web browser and navigate to Google.com.

> In the search place for Google, type in "find my Android."

Once you type this in, Google is ready to assist you with finding your Android Phone.

> Tap get started located at the bottom of the result page, as shown in the picture below.

> Choose the Device you wish to find.

On the next page, you'll see a listing of mobile devices with your Google account logged in. Click on the one you wish to find.

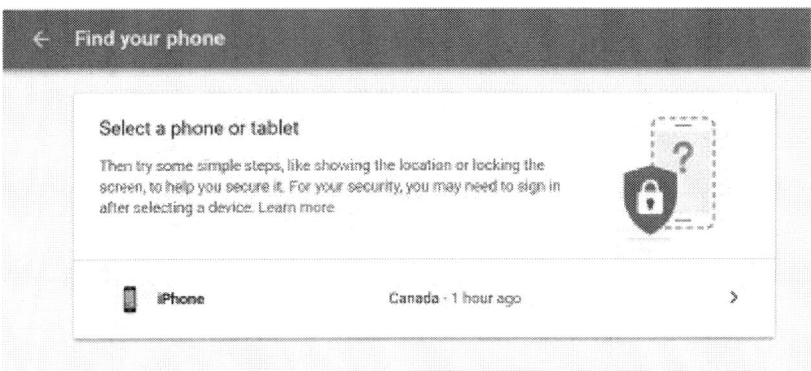

> Log into your Google account.

Now, you'll get to sign up for your Google account. Enter your email address and your password to log in.

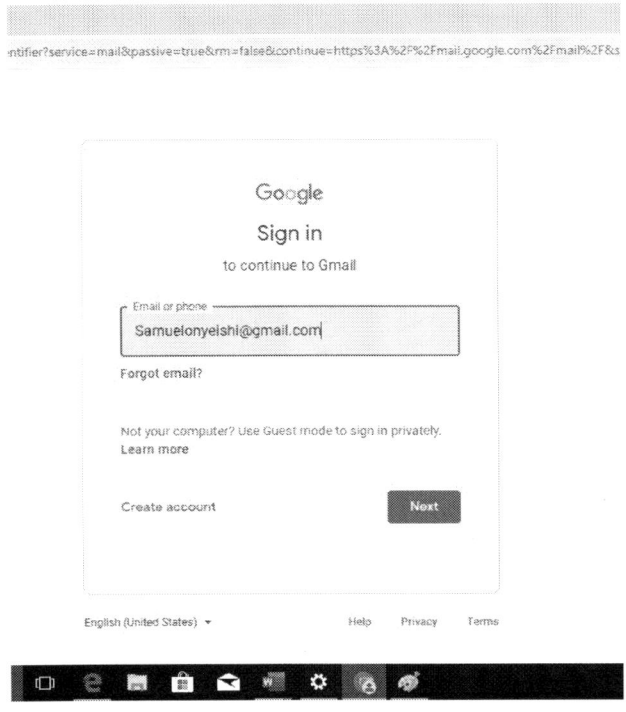

➢ Follow the directions on your screen to find your Android device.

Once you've signed into your Google account, you'll see a listing of choices for ways you can find your Device. You can apply any of them and log out of your account (for privacy's sake).

You can make use of the find my Device Android App.
How will the 'find my Device app' work? This is probably what you will be wondering. Before I get to that part, I was hoping you could permit me to talk about what it means to find your Android Phone.

What does find My Device entails?

Find My Device is a type of App for Android devices that enables you to search out your lost Android Phone, tablet, or Android smartwatch. With this App, your Device will create a sound to assist you in finding it, and it even permits you to indicate a message or remotely lock your Device; therefore, no one will be allowed to access your info.

If you would like to get started with using the find my Device app, here are ways to do it:

Enabling the Find My Device

1. Visit the Google play store app on your Android Phone to open it: The first step is to access the Android app store, Google Play.

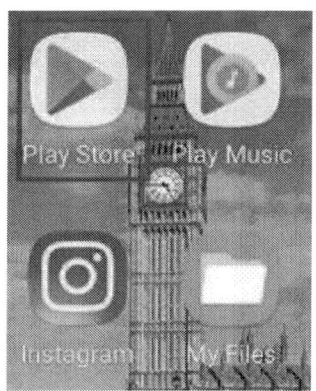

2. Please search for the find my Device App and install it.

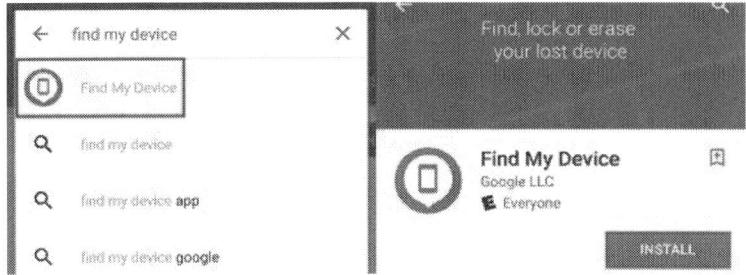

3. Log in with your Google account: Use your Google account details to log into the Find my Device App. This makes it straightforward to use, as you won't have to bother memorizing a new password.

4. Permit the App to access your location and your data: When asked, ensure you permit the App to access your site and contacts. Your location must help the App find your Phone, and your contact information is also needed. Therefore, the App will access the email you've connected with your Google account.

5. Set your Device to permit remote protection and erasing of information: To allow the App to lock or erase your device remotely, you'll have to make changes to your phone settings. To do so, tap your phone settings.

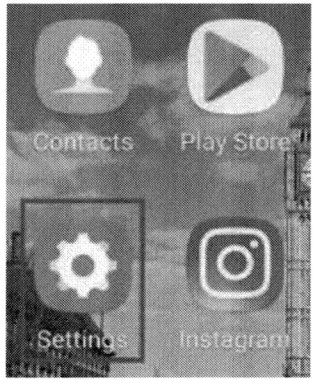

Choose Google

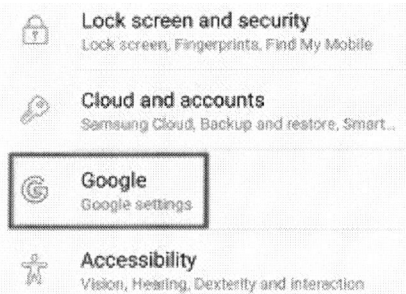

Tap 'sign-in & security'

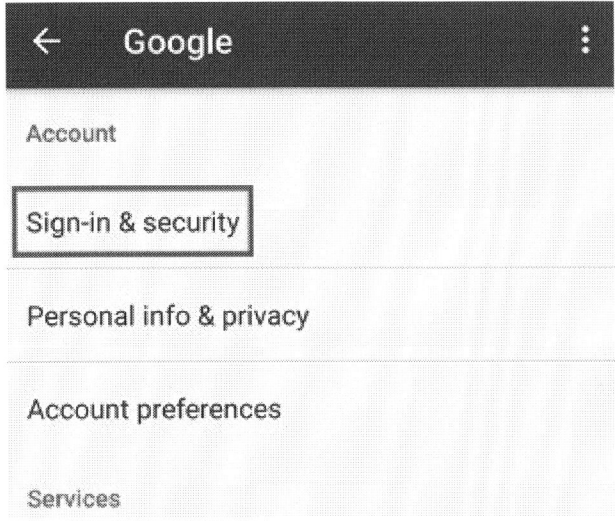

Finally, you can change the feature by tapping on the slider that is labeled "Allow Remote Lock and Erases."

6. You can do a test run to ensure everything was adequately set up.

Try out the App and confirm that you have set it up the right way it should be.

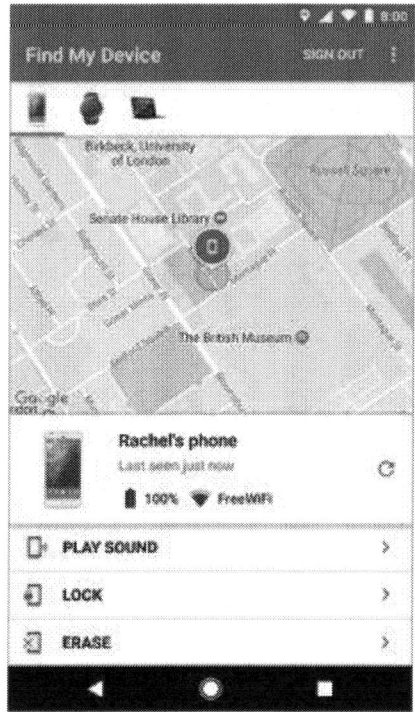

Those six steps are all you need to set the 'find my device' App. With them, you can locate your Device wherever it is. Now, let's get into how you can use the App to find your missing Android Phone.

How to find your Android Phone with the 'Find My Device app.'

If you have misplaced your Android Phone and will like to find it, log into the 'find my device' App on a laptop and perform the following actions:

1. Open your preferred web browser and visit the 'find My Device' website.

2. Log in to your Google account.

Using your email address and password, sign in to your Google Account

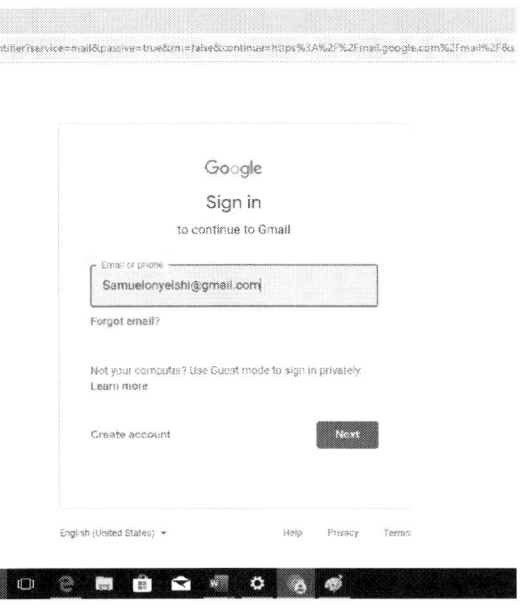

3. Choose the Device you want to search out from the highest part of your screen.

At the top-left corner of your screen, you will see a listing of devices you've paired with the App. Click on the one you're attempting to find.

4. You can make use of any of the options available on the website. The options include: lock your Device, play a sound, and so many others. Once you've selected what you will like to do, it will automatically do your bidding. And if your Phone should be stolen, the erase all information will help you protect your information.

This is all for the second technique for finding your lost Phone. Though this technique requires you to install an app, it is still very efficient and suitable for retrieving lost phones.

Since we are now speaking of apps for retrieving your lost phones, there are many apps with which you can find your lost phones. I will like to show you a few of these apps, they include:

The 'Family locator' App

The family locator app is an app with which you can keep track of your Android Phone, and it is additionally lovely for families, friend teams, etc., who want to keep track of each other's location. You have to create an inner circle of people, and you will all monitor each other's background and even chat in the App.

You can set it to notify you once somebody in your Circle arrives or leaves a given destination, e.g., school or your workplace, and you can even see where they're on a map. This App may be an excellent way to keep your treasured ones safe and locate devices after getting lost or taken.

The 'Prey Anti-Theft'

This App is a very excellent choice when it comes to keeping track of your Android Phone. You can install it on your PC laptops as well, and it can protect and track over three devices.

The things you can do with the App include:

- See the current location of your devices on a map.

- Set up security alarms that are capable of going off even if your phone volume is low.

- It can lock your Phone.

- You can have access to your phone camera, and you can discretely take pictures to find out who is in current possession of your Phone.

FREQUENTLY ASKED QUESTIONS OF ANDROID USERS

1. How do I add a brand-new email account?

You will likely log into your account when you first power on your Android smartphone or tablet. However, we've multiple email addresses that we'd prefer to manage from our mobile Device for several people. Be it Yahoo!, Hotmail, or another personal account, adding a brand new one is not any downside.

In most instances, the fastest way to add another account is to open the Settings App on your Device. Scroll to Accounts, and you will see a choice to "Add New." From there, it's a matter of putting in your credentials and watching it load.

Some Android versions might not be accessible; however, rest assured, its obscurity is not as difficult as it sounds. Many apps, like Gmail, let users add new accounts directly from the App itself. If you have to add a Google account like Gmail, Google Apps to your email, you may also see an equivalent account elsewhere on the Device. This often includes, but is not restricted to, Google

Play, YouTube, Google Play Music, and Google Books. Once you can use your Phone flawlessly, you will be able to manually modify the settings on your account. You will additionally move into and manually adjust set settings on your accounts.

2. Where do I find apps and games?

A brand-new phone can feature an icon to get your Google Play on your home screen.

If you have created an account earlier, then you are good to go. If it turns out that you can't see the Google Play icon on your screen, then you need to open up the app receptacle, which is usually an icon that appears like tiny squares at the lowest of your Phone. Scroll through your app list till you see Google Play, and there you go! with one tap, you're off to transfer new and marvelous apps.

3. How do I uninstall apps or games?

So, you downloaded a game you kept hearing about, or an app you feel is the best, and now you have lost interest in it. If you are new to using an Android phone, you will probably wonder what to do now. The answer to that is "Uninstall it." No sense in keeping an app on your Phone takes up your storage space and slows down the processing of your Phone.

To uninstall an Android app or game, head to your app receptacle. Scroll till you reach the Settings App and go to the Application

Manager, Apps, or anything similar, since it may not be the same for all Android phones.

Generally, you will notice that each one of your apps will be listed in alphabetical order. Tap on the App you wish to uninstall and tap uninstall.

You will see other options like force stop, and the force stop option automatically stops the App.

4. How do I alter the wallpaper?

Would you prefer to alter the background image on your Phone to something completely different? That's a straightforward thing to do, and there are several ways to do that.

The first method to use in changing your wallpaper is:

> ➤ Tap and hold your screen for some seconds to see if a menu screen will come up.

If that doesn't work, then you will have to move to the following method.

> ➤ Open your app tray, which is the icon that looks like small squares and is located at the bottom of your Phone. Look for an option for 'Display' and toggle through the settings. That is where you will make any adjustment you want to your display.

5. Are my photos mechanically saved to Google Photos?

If you would like Google Photos to Backup mechanically, you will have to make some minor changes to your settings. The Google Photos app is intended to avoid wasting battery life and cellular information. Therefore, wireless local area network and background permissions are set as a default.

Instead of WLAN, to Backup over cellular information,

- ➤ Open the Google Photos app and tap on the profile icon within the higher right-hand corner.

- ➤ Next, tap on App Settings and toggle the Cellular information possibility.

- ➤ Next, go into your Phone'sPhone's settings and toggle the background battery usage for Google photos.

- ➤ Now, Google Photos ought to mechanically backup all your photos.

6. How do I retrieve my pictures from Google Photos?

Once everything is insured, accessing your photos is simple. All you would do is open the Google Photos app and check-in mistreatment identical Gmail account everything is saved to.

Once logged in, you ought to see all of your photos within the Google Photos app. Tap on a picture or album and tap the share icon to send the photographs to a different person or put it aside in other places.

7. Can I save all Google Photos to my Phone at once?

Yes, you can save all of your photos to your Google photos at once. To do this:

- ➢ Long-press a photograph to initiate the choice to pick all of the pictures you need to avoid wasting time.

- ➢ Then, tap the Android share icon to keep all photos on your Phone.

- ➢ Using the Android share icon, you can save them to your Device or share the photos with another cloud service or contacts.

8. How do I add a new contact?

One of the good options we tend to come to, like in Android's initial build, was the cloud-based contact system. You can now forget about losing track of names and numbers on your smartphones. It will arrange everything for you, your friends, and your family would be kept in one spot, accessible and synchronous all over. Things have evolved, and currently, you can have multiple phone numbers, emails, and social networking profiles.

Your Android contact can be created by heading to your app drawer and tap on the Contacts App.

Another way to make a brand-new contact is to travel into the phone application. Tap and hold your home screen for some to see if a menu screen comes up. If a menu comes up, you will see the option to modify or create a new contact.

An Android phone user should use Gmail or Google+ to manage their contacts. Since Google owns the operating system, using all its services will be a great plus to your user experience.

9. How do I toggle Wi-Fi, Bluetooth, etc.?

It is excellent for you to have Wi-Fi, GPS, or Bluetooth running on your devices, but it is not necessary at all times. You will have to neglect them at certain times to maximize your battery life. Early and existing versions of Android provide quick access for toggling your connections and choices through the settings.

> Open the app tray, and you will see the primary things there, you will see the wireless and network settings, and you will be able to turn on/off the Wi-Fi with a single tap.

New versions of Android have a dropdown menu from the notification bar, which you may access by swiping your right-hand side. Finally, there's an opportunity that you just may also hit the menu button on the home screen of your Android to reveal settings.

10. How do I examine if there's an Android update?

Maybe you purchased your Android telephone set secondhand. Perhaps you've switched devices over time and will be returning to your initial smartphone. Regardless of the case, you would like to ascertain if there is an update that is accessible at that moment.

Each Device could be a bit completely different; however, several use equivalent ways for code and updates. If you have done an update before, then you will be able to do it,

> ➢ Open your app tray, in several cases, and you will scroll to the bottom of the menu till you see a System update or something like that. Your Phone is intended to check for updates. Thus, sporadically, you will see one thing that references the last time it looked for an update. Potentially, you can also see references to code, software, profiles, PRL, or general Android updates.

11. How to lock your Android Phone

If you have things of importance to you, it'd be a drag if it got into the hands of others. Even if you don't have something important, it'd still be a drag if somebody were to get you into your Phone. What does one do to combat prying eyes, to a jealous lover, or snooping colleagues? The simple thing to do is to put a security lock in place.

I'm not talking of a 3rd party app or some deep-level security on your Phone, and it is just a simple barrier to keep unwanted people away. Android offers various security screen choices that provide users peace of mind, adding new and innovative stuff to the method. You are allowed to use a pattern unlock, PIN, face recognition, watchword, or a mixture of things.

> ➢ Open your app tray, and your expertise can vary, counting on manufacturer and version of Android; but, by looking around, you can see one that indicates a lock. Once you're in there, you will see settings for the various ways of locking your Phone.

Feel free to play around along with your lock screen choices; however, don't forget your password. Also, it is best to keep some of your information on the lock screen. This way, a good-deed-doer who picks your Phone will be able to locate you and give it to you.

12. Do you wish to add an icon to your house screen?

Early versions of Android made it easy for users to add an app icon/shortcut by simply long pressing, tapping, and holding your screen for a few seconds. The same was applicable for widgets. Later versions of Android changed things by putting widgets in your app tray. When you go to the app tray, you will see an option to add or remove widgets.

Another way to add something to your home screen is to open the app tray and scroll until you see the App or widget you wish to put on your screen. Tap and hold it for few seconds and drag it to your home screen. You can then place it where you prefer.

13. How do I modify my screen brightness?

- Open the app tray and scroll till you see Settings.

- Once in there, you will come upon a tab or menu choice for brightness or show. HTC, as an example, lists this underneath show & gesture. On the other hand, Samsung can usually place the slider directly within the dropdown that is accessible by swiping down from the notification bar.

- You can slide the brightness up and down and manually to set things, but it is best to put it to auto-adjust. Do not let your screen be too bright to maximize your battery life.

The major setbacks of Android phones

No operating system is entirely perfect, there are bound to minor issues which can be insignificant, and the Android operating system is not exceptional to this. Despite all the amazing features and all the benefits, you gain from using the Android operating system, there are still some inconsistencies due to the large number of people who make Android devices. Two android phones of similar kind can do two totally different things, they might even seem unrelated, all because of the presence of different Android versions. But these is not a major issue because Android keeps creating room for users to update their version of the operating system. So, the decision to use an older version when there is an availability of a newer version, is totally left to you.

Another major issue with the Android operating system is that it gives its users the freedom to download any app and to share apps and other files with different people. This can be seen as a disadvantage and an advantage. The disadvantage being that your Android phones are exposed to potential malware that can steal your important information.

Battery life

The Android operating system is not known to maximize the battery life of its users, but over the years there have been a major improvement in the battery duration. There are Android phones who now have battery capacity of over 6000mah, which is a major improvement compared to other operating systems.

Conclusion

Android is more customizable and versatile than 'iOS' which is the iPhone operating system, making it irresistible. This book is designed to help you get the best out of your Android Phone, regardless of your level of knowledge. In this book, I have covered all the basic and complex operations you can do with your android phone.

You will be more than glad you came across this book.

Manufactured by Amazon.ca
Bolton, ON